T0317110

GOODNIGHT **ARCHITECTURE**

New Issues Poetry & Prose

Editor	Herbert Scott
Associate Editor	David Dodd Lee
Advisory Editors	Nancy Eimers, Mark Halliday, William Olsen, J. Allyn Rosser
Assistants to the Editor	Rebecca Beech, Lynnea Page, Derek Pollard, Jonathan Pugh, Marianne E. Swierenga
Assistant Editors	Kirsten Hemmy, Erik Lesniewski, Adela Najarro, Margaret von Steinen
Editorial Assistant	Jennifer Abbott
Business Manager	Michele McLaughlin
Fiscal Officer	Marilyn Rowe

New Issues Poetry & Prose
The College of Arts and Sciences
Western Michigan University
Kalamazoo, MI 49008

First Edition, 2002.

| ISBN | 1-930974-21-3 (paperbound) |

Library of Congress Cataloging-in-Publication Data:
Mattox, Gretchen
Goodnight Architecture/Gretchen Mattox
Library of Congress Control Number: 2002104232

Art Direction	Joseph Wingard
Design	Christine Coller
Additional Photography	Sarah Peltzie ("This is")
Production	Paul Sizer
	The Design Center, Department of Art
	College of Fine Arts
	Western Michigan University

GOODNIGHT ARCHITECTURE

GRETCHEN MATTOX

New Issues

WESTERN MICHIGAN UNIVERSITY

for Terence
for Jocko

Contents

I

The Field 9

The Olive Tree 10

Demane and Demazana 12

The Psychic's Daughter 14

Elegy (Divine Mother, the garden black) 15

The Pheasant 16

Escape (Fragment) 18

In the aerial dream of water 19

Confidence Not to Hear Sorrow 20

The Babies 21

Goodnight Architecture 22

Elegy (The woods sodden with milk) 24

Country of No Words 25

Libation Bowl with Acorns and Bees 26

Office Visit 27

Wood Bone Body 29

Light on the Lower Body 31

Albeit 32

Elegy (In the middle of my life) 34

The Father 35

Mother of the Waters 36

Elegy (sadness in vistas be birth now) 37

II

Fire on Charles Street   41

Denver 1977   42

The Hanging Gardens   43

A Basket in Which Fish Are Carried   44

The Hermaphrodite's Daughter   45

Drunk in Provincetown   46

Separation   47

Elegy (What I asked was)   49

The Wasps' Nest   50

Floribundus Passage   51

Conversant Water   52

Larger Sea   53

Slicing Beets   54

White-Tailed Deer Feeding   55

Elegy (Leaving the marriage)   56

Resilience   57

Quotidian   58

After Marriage   59

White Torch   60

Elegy (We trawl the lake)   61

Elegy (The morning is a buried place)   62

Safety and Memory   63

Variation on Seeing: A Prayer   64

Everywhere   65

Love Poem to My Grandmother   67

Building and Dwelling   69

Revelatory Borders   71

Notes   73

Acknowledgments

Thank you to the editors of the following journals in which these poems originally appeared, some of them in different versions:

American Poetry Review: "A Basket in Which Fish Are Carried," "Elegy (We trawl the lake)," "Elegy (What I asked was)," "Elegy (The woods sodden)," "Quotidian"

Ark: "Albeit"

Columbia Magazine: "Libation Bowl with Acorns and Bees"

Eclipse: "After Marriage"

Fishdrum: "Separation"

Many Mountains Moving: "Country of No Words," "The Pheasant"

Mudfish: "Conversant Water," "The Field"

The North American Review: "Demane and Demazana"

Pequod: "The Hanging Gardens," "The Olive Tree," "Floribundus Passage"

Ploughshares: "Mother of the Waters"

Salt: "Escape (Fragment)"

I would like to gratefully acknowledge the unwavering support of Nicole Cooley, Elizabeth Lapin, Deborah Landau, Dana Levin, Amy Schroeder, Judith Taylor, Heidi Vogel and, of course, Jocko in bringing this book to fruition. A special thank you in bold neon to David Dodd Lee for his selfless dedication to poetry and his keen editorial eye. Heartfelt gratitude is extended to my natal and spiritual families, as well as my many teachers, both fellow poets and/or fellow travelers. Thank you to the Edward Albee Foundation, the Virginia Center for the Creative Arts, Yaddo, New York University, and Columbia University.

I

. . . You spoke of "Hope" surpassing "Home"—I thought that Hope was Home—a misapprehension of Architecture—but then if I knew . . .
—Emily Dickinson

The Field

I am dreaming of the caustic smoke of the father behind the father.
There is a pear on the table in unfathomable light.

You are not safe in your white dress.
What is all this nonsense about vision?

Do you think self-abuse is noble?
That the field of a thousand breasts can bring the world to focus?

When my father hung himself in the bathroom,
his feet swelled like the heads of crowning infants.

Fire heralded across the field, all hiss and pantomime.
Years ago, I got up and walked away.

Everything burns, the outstretched hand, memory, the dress?
Here, console yourself, look back and tell.

The Olive Tree

O mythical father,
keep your eyes bandaged shut,
there's nothing to contend with here.

I have agreed to bury the daughter for both of us,
to walk askance pelted by sorrow and light
as indeterminate wind pocks my face.

I know you will refute how difficult it's been.
Once I sat at your feet
before the table of the universe

and asked you to take my life.
You didn't answer so I thought you cared.
You drunk. How could I have known exhaustion

would lead you again and again through the revolving door
of unopened letters dissolving like shrouds
with the seasons—each angle of light—

until it is dark, darker than ever,
not a star to be wished upon?
After many nights we reached

a burning in the shape of a body within a body.
I forgot who I was,
each rose bud became a face wrapped in placenta,

open window, a catch phrase,
many daughters sat on a fence
with their skirts hiked up,

blossoms rose from the trees like clouds.
Don't you think I heard you and heard you and heard you?
Under the cinema moon

wolf tracks embossed the snow;
from here we could make out
the city of gold, the lambs' heads displayed on plates,

the touch disassociated from touch.
In a series of accidents
I cut my finger with intention

and looked behind me to see
the road completely disappear.
If pollen from the olive tree inflames your lungs,

take out an axe and do away with it.

Demane and Demazana

Demazana, Demazana, Child of my mother, Open this cave to me.
The swallows can enter it. It has two openings.

—African folk tale

i.
Swallows came and left, leaves in wind.
Sister, I know you hungered.
The cave you wore like being
inside a body all over again.
Abiding moon or not, we were parentless.
You cooked buffalo meat on the fire
and the fat spat back its own accusations.
It was hard to tell who to trust.
Light exonerated you through two air holes.
So you let him in. He'll be a tree stuffed with bees soon enough.
Metaphor of sexual deflowering.
I gained strength from your poor choices;
the price of rebellion was a life.
The sky is a loud blue.
A bee sits on your elbow. Let me flick it off.

ii.
Excess honey licked from the finger,
a lie built to confine desire. How unfair to watch
a compilation of powers expressed in you
and be denied them, swarm of bees in the shape of a man
running down a road, too much contention, too much violence;
he couldn't have me, but you can?
One stung my lip, another my left ear.
I shrugged it off, the low hum of agitation, totem and regret.
It made me wet, just thinking of what we would never do.

iii.
Hand-rolled pottery coiled like diamondbacks under shadows;
in a moment of sexual recognition, I am made whole
by your desire and the fear of mine.
This is what separates us.
Bees like small engines of absolute rage
pursued us down the hill back to the cave.
We were rich by then with sacks of gold
the virtuous are promised.
You know, it was never a matter of saving me.
I was out of breath. It could not be helped;
desire's momentum shook us free from our senses.
You removed the stinger, obsequious tattoo,
splinter, subordinate indiscretion, my hand in your hand,
caution flower, raspberry welt, the glorious swelling.
We dry-humped on the ground.
I held back and so did you.
In the hammock of woven vine, we slept as brother and sister,
desire stuck in a fissure of the self;
night came like an accomplice to promise, to abandonment;
the moon, cold as another country, split your face in twos.
I made myself come just looking at you.

The Psychic's Daughter

i.
At night the souls creep out.
When I call you, father, you shut me up.
Best to walk a few feet above ground, best to commune out of body.
In our collective mind I see the kidney-shaped pools of childhood,
Light bracken moving over highways and spores.
Everywhere asking more of me than I know to be possible.
It goes on and on; eyes under the bed illumined as pyrite.
Please be good. Please forgive.

ii.
In my dream of the Red Sea you are waist-deep in water
Wearing a suit and bow tie. As the crystal ball clouds,
Small mechanical blue jays multiply, outdistancing every intention;
What you know you don't speak of. I am not of this world, either.
The furies, the already dead, the ones
With their tongues in hand group around me.

iii.
The wind eddied, and wind chimes—atonal, peripheral—
Tapped the silence like ice in a glass.
The sky made us see more than we wanted.
That's the risk we all take. Do you think you're special?

iv.
The blindfolded girl speaking of cities
Sustained wholly by light is my sister.
We can go there without a father. I know it.
Someone other than you will tell me.
When I think of the word *gauze*, death-mask comes to mind.
The days are so hot. We are in the thick of summer.
In the only photograph I have of you, your expression is liquid,
        hard to make out,
As if the spirits are already behind us,
Predicting murders, warning of fire, finding lost keys.

Elegy

Divine Mother, the garden of black flowers tucked away like a dowry
resembles the myth of closed eyes, the blind only pretending to see.
My sexual reflection trampled with both feet
is locked in a little box.

Then I fall forgetting you.

Memory travels outside my body. I cling to pieces of earth at every step.
Simultaneously, the light of emptying
turns to dwelling.

The Pheasant

When my father came home he put the pheasant on top of the
        washing machine.
It was limp at the neck. I smelled fabric softener and blood
as the dryer rotated like a mandala.
Outside, snow hurried over Pullman, Washington.
I wasn't allowed to touch it, in case it had a disease.
My father the gynecologist knew about diseases.
He had books of women whose hormones had gone berserk,
naked women made anonymous by the black rectangle across
        their eyes, a blindfold.
They were strip-search victims with hanging breasts.
Then the dream came: the women face down in the mud.
Are you going to spend your whole life feeling inadequate?
Whose voice? I couldn't locate it, not if it meant more grief.
They were so beautiful and damaged, I named them *eternity*
to keep myself from becoming one of them.
The dream was grainy and I threw stones at its surface
to prove how competent I was, to prove I was not the girl
        anymore who'd watched
the pheasant's blood streak the white and shiny appliance.
My father and the fathers before him, reflected in the various
        veils of form,
are the frozen pillars in a temple around us.
The darkness is a guest that pushes against the ongoing lack.
At each turn, the road asked to be translated.
I leaned on the dryer, trying to find the bullet hole.
Where did it go in and where did it come out?
The emerald band at the neck was metaphysical.
It looked medieval, too, like those still-life paintings with
        cornucopias and pewter goblets.
I didn't touch it. I didn't want to touch it, not if touching
        meant to disobey, meant sickness.
I repeated my first breath over and over, stuck, having to
        infer *absence*.

My father took off his boots, washed his hands, popped open a beer.
The women sing into the dark as if nothing is wrong.
I have been taught to ignore their voices and I do not hear them.

Escape (fragment)

i.
When the first angel looked away, I could see myself running a foot
        above ground, unable to touch down.
The room felt like a room just emptied after a large party. From a
        storm in the Midwest my brother
called to say he loved me and I heard noise like stones rubbing
        together. A yellow bird, no bigger than a
fingernail, flew from the equator to the center of a movie screen.
        What was left but expanse drifting
like an unmanned boat?

ii.
Then the light beings without bodies appeared in legions.
                And so in the evening undone like a bridge
        between matter and spirit, I dreamed
in degrees the vague attachments like peripheral vision—catching
        what?—out of
the corner of my eye.

There were various stars, some rapture in the broad sea of lit candles.

In the aerial dream of water and sky—stratus of differentiated blues—the ocean is like a dream of itself, veils of light and a vastness. Later, many yellow flowers and the neighbor's cat walking the rail of the fence, his tail like a fin moving above the brushline.

Confidence Not to Hear Sorrow

i.
It must have tasted like grief, the narrative flame. Nothing fit again,
a miscalculation of weather.

Succulents turned like listening ears to the light, kin to artichokes.

Small kindnesses were a film of water over water, the drop caught
for how long exactly?

And if love was to begin, I needed edges.

It must have tasted like salt—possibility beyond my view.
Clouds, cool light, white curtains shredded with flames.

ii.
What the earth yielded; dirt giving way to cypress, medieval trees
of walled cities, towering
and groomed. The succulents—aloe vera, maybe—like speakers on
old victrolas.

And it was love, wasn't it, that made us explicit in our bodies?

Everything calling out to something else.

The Babies

The aborted babies are happy.
If they had faces they would smile
but their skins are slick as blisters.
They live in limbo among many worlds,
where trees call out *Andante!*
They do not want to clap and sing like the other kids,
preferring the dark universe of their mothers' bodies.
Who can blame them?
We can almost see the doctor suck
the microscopic oyster-sack into the operating light.
Their souls transmigrate like colors in paintings.
Theirs is the beauty of Rome
and all that I cannot answer,
as stalagmites in a cave, a beauty
that proffers from dark.
The small heads of aborted babies
are silent as cherry tomatoes
sitting in boxes outside the market.
The unborn wait for the boatman, with oars slender
as prepubescent daughters, to ferry them away from
mothers they will never know.

Goodnight Architecture

i.
When I hold the dead girl, the small of her back locates me
while all around us lilies breathe their toxic sweetness
and grasses move in wind like cilia.
The midnight exhausted with stars is from a previous eon.
Voices of sheets decompose us into pure consciousness.
God does not live here.
The gutted buds expose themselves
as slaughtered animals on the lawn.
I do not want to huddle before the fever together.
Go ahead, cop out on me.
In a dormant lullaby, trees narrate otherness and sky and a hand
                touching the brow.
I am not lost, dear one.
We can love the life back into each other—even from this distance.
The long neck of childhood is only shadow feeding upon shadow;
a subtext of origins. How could I have been so stupid?
You were no more my mother than I yours.

ii.
Whatever I needed to know, I have gone on without.
Even the clasped bodies of lovers
turning and turning in sheets
(is the world art?) will pause for the light's perfunctory look.
Perhaps the door breaks a subtler silence.
Like an underwater language from my hand to yours,
the morning ignites us.
My mother stands on the far bank near the bed.
In unison, two little girls say, *hold me*.
Burnt-out trees appear prehistoric.
Can anything live there?
In one dominion, I never reach her

and in another I never leave.
A black dog that won't let anyone touch it follows me.
The disinterested urn is stuck in the dirt.
Whatever I touch turns to grief.

Elegy

The woods sodden with milk;
I have come to want hunger.
Faraway my mother instructs me on repose.

And on the hill, the boxed clouds:
how *apart from* there is no rest.

The woods sodden with milk.
The complaint industrial.
The encouraged helplessness.

My mother's secret: she is still a child.
It begins in subterfuge, but always ends in envy.
How slowly the prophesy drifts to my door,
until I am utterly certain
happiness is a parable lettered in ropes and shadows.

Country of No Words

i.
When he sent that thrust of cum into her
the smell of estuaries overwhelmed me
across the miles. Defiance and lies.
I became invisible with shame
like lamp light exhausted in a sun-blind field.
I set up house in the country of no words
where suffering and desire lock horns
like gazelles bounding in our mutual sleep.

The most adorable girl
with a pixie haircut keeps waiting
by the door for her father.

ii.
I saw the small boy in my husband
who'd watched his mother
naked, drunk, slice her forearm
into bloody cuneiform
and get carted off to the sanitarium—
how he'd raised himself, alone
on will; the way all things
innately turn to living.

iii.
Though it's been a year or more
I still want to know her name.
I feel close to her
as if I was the one to spread her legs
as if we'd fucked her together
in a pact to release us
from the silence we agreed to keep
such a long time ago.

Libation Bowl with Acorns and Bees

4th Century B.C.

I am the joy where rivers assert a singular present
and you who traded reciprocity for a slap cannot find me.
Dead bees clog the libation bowl but the gods do not mind.
All that I know about trust was decided in this dim collinear heat.
Peonies, in a neglected garden made of ash, break apart dusk,
it is memory or injury like a nick in birch bark. *You loved me*
            more than . . . ?
Carbon doves struggle with their angular wings.
They make such fools of themselves.
I'd send them into flight but their wings cannot withstand the
            supposition of height.
Shadows bear insular, intricate fruit which I am unable to swallow.

Office Visit

The last time I saw him that year, he stood in his white hospital coat
and stethoscope under a painting of the Austrian Alps
next to charts covering *menses*.
He explained to his fifteen-year-old daughter,
An affair is only a symptom of an already bad marriage.
I looked down at my wrist, the veins, the lateral bruises, a path
        of bruises.
I knew who she was.
It took months for the fetus to resemble a baby.
Finally, upside down in the universe of the womb,
eyes shut, the skin magnified, coated with amniotic fluid and the
        sloughed-off cells like salt,
sucking its thumb in the stellar expanse, an expression, human.
My father went on, something about love and custody.
I had heard her name, long after the arguments, the shouting,
        the accusations.
She was like the women with perfect nails in evening gowns
who walk panthers and advertise diamonds on TV.
We left my father in the house on Mohawk Drive
with a view of Mt. Rainer and became statistics.
It was hard to believe I was really his daughter once,
having been sent to Denver
with just a few boxes of stuff.
I was being turned into a woman against my will.
My breasts felt fat, extemporaneous. Suddenly, I had hips
and cramps and no one to go to.
My father, the expert on female development, was gone.
He knew how the body worked.
I hid my breasts under oversized sweaters
and walked the supermarket aisles
looking for Dexatrim, diet pills, diuretics, ex-lax.
The best pills were pink, fluorescent, the color of feminine happiness.
Every night I got in bed and prayed to lose five more pounds.
How could God ignore me?
I understood you were tired of being a father,

that the women in your life had taken and taken
and I was part of the taking, never giving back;
conceived before marriage, I'd pushed you into it
when I was lost to an interior sky, sex undetectable.

Wood Bone Body

i

What I took to be of grave concern hardly mattered. The light
        was sand filling our mouths.
Do I displease you? The scattered infusion of palm trees that
        polka-dot the horizon. What do you want
me to divulge?

I was steering the boat of my concern beyond a certain agitation.

Like sitting in a tree as *girl* while a bee—drunkard of air, there
        caught in my longing

I'd pushed away—stung me anyway.
Horror wasn't the wood / bone / body sliver but my inability to
        avoid pain.

Now the California landscape unfolds itself. Evade me.

ii.

The storm quelled but we were uneasy with left-over malice and
        the many lakes still shoved
under darkening skies by this I mean restoration of balance /
        tremble of cups / jostle of water.

Here are my cells like stars. Here is my blood and the one tooth
        left in my mouth.
Tumbleweeds roll barbed wire don't even try.

iii.

Eternity and all the whys like yapping dogs how gladly I would
        have rendered all the loss useless, my
father's twenty-year absence no longer *his* but the absence of
        archetype (I stumble), his climbing into
unassailable air and in me that protected absence concave as
        the punch in rising bread.

iv.
Dispensable—even though the moon dazzled its heartfelt thanks.
        Less was the defining order. Less
than less. Did it give you a fist to shake? Was it a walking stick?
        Did it lift you above the clutter?

v.
My jeweled brooch, this morning a bee walks the back of the sofa.

Light on the Lower Body

Divine Mother, mirror of earth and air
this is the ruin of despondency,
what the boys did, taking me in their parents' cars.
The steep slope the vertical decline of sexual becoming;
a wash of purple buds, hillside and I am falling.
This is the landscape blown up by dreams and astral light.
I was unworthy of my own desire
so I let them do what they wanted; it *seemed* love-like, maybe better.
Blood and dirt—of blood and dirt
the sexual river taking me with it
until I wanted only a diffusion of my own existence.
Passion flower in the garden of girls,
there was ash on my tongue as I took their cocks in my mouth.
The moon flared through time.
How else could I go on?
Sixteen—working at McDonald's selling fries.
The air filled with opposing heavens.
S. pushing me against the rec room wall
by the red bean bag chair and the colonial print hide-a-bed.
Light on the lower body.
The year, audible beneath the brightness. Confirming my thirst.
Only desire—their strong arms, my breasts yielding and new
—meeting after school while our parents worked.
The sexual river taking me with it.
K. in his Datsun 280Z, tiny envelopes of cocaine.
We agreed like veterans in the hollow of our almost adulthood
          to use each other.
When I lost it, S. and I skipped school and sat poolside
eating peanut butter and jelly sandwiches,
the hard jargon of lust and the smell of sex between us.
Later as the griefs gathered around me, I told no one.

Albeit

What was definitive
wore a red dress.
We were stunned
as naturally we should have been
when the hands that had been
after our ankles like sea anemones
began waving *hi* and the light
made crooked by the crags
turned narrow as the ABC's.

We were walking along the wharf
out to where two fisherman arced their poles
by a yellow bucket of bait,
pot of scintillating coins held up to heaven
(the smallest of offerings are the most . . .).

That I heard singing
(from a choir of nuns descending the stairs
on a nearby hillside; the brass banister
clear as a bell by the sketches of branches)
made no difference,
not to the red dress or the fish bait.

It came out in me as kicking a clod of dirt,
scribbling curlicues in the air . . .
Once I saw a man write his name in snow
while taking a piss.
It stayed with me.
It came to comfort me.
Because I knew how small we were.

The pert purple blooms of water hyacinth
choking the channels of the Gulf, *beautiful*
beneath the cattails and marsh grass.
We look out with a long reach on a split sky

as the water, a mind clear of thought,
tempts us to walk out even farther.
Behind us the sun emblazoned on the neighborhood
is an orange spot going down.
A hand reaches inside, pulling out
bright scarf after scarf.

Elegy

In the middle of my life I followed the random fires
of solo fallout straight to the radius of my fear.

For luck, I took your hand with me.
Something in the eternal sea wanted to be sealed off.

What mindlessness I couldn't love in you
I've had to accept in myself.

Autumn mouths its flares of sickness or blood,
each turning leaf a cellular icon.

Closure is not indifference, or, put another way,
it's more difficult to go back than on.

The Father

What would it be like to forgive my father?
We hoped he would come back to us, maybe a little broken.

Mother of the Waters

I live by the river, daughter to no one.
Of course, I want. The formless sea fills every window,
always the sleeping gift in my left hand, not how the life was outlined.
The underwater road is obscured, as it should be. Light years waste
        away in my body.
When my mistress sends me to wash the silver,
one silver teaspoon catches in the current, slips from my fingers.

I cross over and come back with my hands folded in prayer.
Mother of the Waters tells me *the black chair, the black room,*
the black map are all invented. She is a sorcerer,
a witch of winds that plays the currents of water and air against
        one another.
It seems important to want what I've been given
until the part about comparison, the part about letting go
becomes a cold spoonful offered up at dusk.

I sit on a rock and cry, a girl of my own making,
join the talk of water and the first mother behind all mothers.
This is how to leave the attenuated miles.
Mother of the Waters says, *Wash my back,* and I do.
Each time I touch her, I am healed.
In a symmetry of motion, clouds open like eggs of light.
I cannot bring her into focus and this is how I recognize her;
her back covered with sores, each cut a misshapen well.

All my life I have been prepared to apologize,
the tightness in the throat, the joy of withholding,
for something I must have done.
Take this bean, take this bone, take this grain of rice, and make us
        something to eat.
Always the same lesson: matter cannot be trusted.
The soup suddenly thick and abundant, more than enough.

Elegy

sadness in vistas be birth now
the canal of water of fluid
loathe your body
red hood, thighs
fish lung, mother keeper, hitched a ride here,
think forgive, not forget,
the pendulum which is our lives swings
in and out of balance
I have never stopped missing you

II

Fire on Charles Street

The fire truck red as a fresh cut rushed up the street.
Can you see how carefully I must hold myself?

We watched smoke rise in a froth from the roof
as flames in a kinetic dance took over the building.

Sirens yelled. And then what?

We could smell the rage burning asphalt and hair.

A man in an aqua T-shirt sat like "The Thinker"
near the ledge of a neighboring window.

I was alone. I was ten. I was thirty. I drank
because I'd already lost what there was to lose.

Now you want me to start over and love again
that which slipped out of reach as a dress sulks to the floor?

O fire I am consumed by selfishness and loss.
Take me as your next random sacrifice. That's how you work, isn't it?

Denver 1977

The girl is so high she can't get off the bathroom floor,
long hair against the white tile like a head underwater.

The literal moment of annihilation

reduced to the pungent
almost rubbery smell of vomit.
A body made of paper.

Do you know her? Do you want to bury her with stones,
build an altar to conceal her body?

Clouds and fish pass between ancient columns assembled in the mind.
The porcelain sink and pipes dewy with water dismiss the moment.

What use was sickness against all that emptiness?

No light warmed you.

Denver is a boom town, the mile-high city of rapid growth.
She chews the acrid mushrooms.

The patois of dirt gone bitter. Strength
as a child is lifted up over a crowd to see the parade.

The day turns sensual as an exposed thigh.
By 5:30 she'll have dinner ready.

The Hanging Gardens

The vase's crack like the demarcation
between continents on a map
only makes us despondent.
There will be no more asking.
The comforts which come in rows will be discarded.
Do you have a problem with that?
Paperwhite blossoms like origami birds
drop their heads before the sky.
Clouds move over the table.
I hold a rock no good for stoning.
That's the trouble with grief,
it is so easy to ignore the insistent music
and love instead each inconsolable petal.

A Basket in Which Fish Are Carried

Do not defend the itinerant speech of the hero;
that boy's crazy.
Just because he knocks, he thinks the door's open.
I know shame follows me, shame for shame, soft call in my ear,
repeated offerings of watered-down milk,
some insane parting of rose petals,
why, when the tight fist of new bloom
is so much more becoming.
I sleep in the coil of one made for mourning.
Eyes of fish, dull as alkaline junk,
my hand running through my hair.
When my father calls out, I know not to answer
—as the hair splits, as the road opens to rut—
don't you see, I turned on myself because I had to.

The Hermaphrodite's Daughter

In the field of rocks each eye has a name.
I remember the blood you fed me, *poor excuse for tenderness*
long after I was grown, the flatness of the landscape,
the moon, slate and confident above us, the only constant.
You wore the usual *falsies* for breasts.
If I was part of that illusion
you made me swear to never speak of it.
Whatever salutation the world affords us leaves me cold,
as the dry winds unearth the arms of daughters,
as the clouds above pass in their ocular chorus,

as the table, empty now full, empty now full,
asserts this domain: *mystic.* I am that lost.
This is the life where I am named after you,
never feeling a part of, always questioning.
Once you held me and I've had to make allowances
for that accident of attachment,
to watch the sands bury me at will
and go on anyway.
Some essential composite claimed you: boy or girl?
In the end action proceeded inaction.

I couldn't walk the line without losing it.
It was idiomatic to ask me to retrace my steps,
to state how I had arrived and to what purpose,
enigmatic, wholesome as fruit.
Had my eyes actually been shut the entire time?
I was your daughter, after all.
Expiate yourself in this moment. More plea than assertion.
What remains can be salvaged like a shadow deflected across a hand.
We don't know it yet, but the sky extends the perimeters of earth
and no matter what I do, day by day, I become you.

Drunk in Provincetown

The gulls like stitches released.
And the drinking, that central organizing principle
—night after night, waxy,

euphoric balm

because in the end it wasn't life
you couldn't take but yourself.

It did not seem possible, please say how.
Mist unfurling.

In the mud of healing—all body.

The groan of the foghorn, the longest, lonely winter
where the shores of the cape reached to the end of land.

You gave up and up;
the struggle was a kind of denial

Please help.

Until light closed in on you like an aperture.

Separation

Figure 1

Because the river was made of hair, I ignored your tendency to
          complete the prayers in
code, as if a kind of violence was all that reached us. I felt a fire
          sear me in two, but left
the house unacknowledged to go to the movies. Black tits fell
          from an old oak and we
buried the afterbirth from the lost and found, under a carriage house.

See how the stars go out when I am afraid, mostly in antithetical glory
          like a single glass of
milk left on the lawn.

Figure 2

In those first weeks of separation, I saw myself surrounded by water
          on the opposite side
of a river, unable to cross, afraid to speak, uncertain how to make it
          back to my life. Yellow-
winged birds picked at the carcass of an ox and offered me pieces of
          flesh, which I blindly
accepted. I was consumed by rigidity, as if to give in to your absence
          was to admit to failure.

Figure 3

Later, men in pin-striped suits walked from your eye to my mind with
          apples on their
heads, a few cupped tropical butterflies, and others propped ladders
          both vertically
and horizontally in unfamiliar identical rooms. A woman from another

century dropped her
hanky on my lap.

Like an embryo drowned in light, I struggled for my becoming, sad in
        all the ways I'd been before
we met. It was hard to tell who we had been together. I watched a
        throng of ants
eat at the mountain of wedding cake while small clocks ticked in
        my blood.

Figure 4

When we laughed together on a balcony overlooking the sea you took
        my face in your hands.
I assume I imagined pillars of light, loss encased us, monopolized us.
        You said, *I have learned*
to live with this and the sky turned monotonous as engine smoke.
        Pearls dropped into the
geometrical distance from my eyes like tears.

Figure 5

Keystone caught in my throat, I reached out to you in the moments
        of final
letting go and suddenly a huge sky opened underneath me. There was
        much confusion,
some hurry to reach resolve; it seemed impossible to move in any
        direction, like a great
weight, only the miraculous could reach, sealed my life.

Elegy

What I asked was to be taken in, not under.
The womb is too quiet. Open the letter and throw it out.

Leave shame in the audiovisual room where memory shadows
        one side of my body,
the one side of my body dreamed in flesh.

Eyes asunder and eyes roundabout; as if in an ongoing self-
        portrait, I break apart to become.
The hole in my forehead, about average, is a reminder of
        ancient seas.

The Wasps' Nest

Dormant, inverted mud hut, stuck muck on the stucco ceiling
        near the back door.
Always half-expecting an explosion of wasps

from the chewed maché; I didn't dare disturb it
coming and going up the stairs into my rented room.

It had the presence of sudden abandonment like the village of
        Pompeii locked in stone lava.

I feared its emptiness
and the way it called to some stopped rage in me,
the place the story trailed off without ending.

Three years in Los Angeles like a dream I only witnessed
—the feeling my life was not my life.

But it was and I was living with strangers, far away
from things recognizable by outdistancing myself.

So when my ex-husband wrote the letter of apology, professing
        grief and concern for his malfeasance, asking to help
out, saying *I'm here if you need me*

I continued to leave the wasps' nest alone. As if
I had no idea who this man was or what he was talking about.

Floribundus Passage

Omen: beetle on its back like an ancient Egyptian scarab,
buried spring of separation, the marriage over.
Against the neighbor's garage like a geyser from the yard, *lilac*.
How returned to myself every minute of every day
even when I didn't *want* that professed cave of digression
              and anger.
Idea as in no accounting for subterfuge and the spilled losses.
Cracked pitcher, I let my essence go, leak away on your behalf.
The ocean beat traffic-like, heard under Long Island,
              far off, pervasive.
Buds were star replicas, a lower heaven, the Midwest
              brought East,
hiding as a child in the dropped bar of a lilac bough.
Infusion of scent from a flower tree, its sturdiness appealed,
not the frail orbit of lilies or the slumped bodies of tulips
              dead overnight.
Fort of greenery and the feeling no one could find me;
the whole bush contained my body.
The tree tilted with bloom, branches so heavy
they bowed to the ground, weighted by their own excess;
made the pain *having* again.
Proof of devastation: I could barely function
and wanted to stop myself from going.
Bush or tree? The lilac stood high as a roof.
Night a hand over my mouth when emptiness moved
              entombed loss ladder back.

Conversant Water

How right to become what I tried to leave.
Only the conversant water is plausible, the rest hardly matters.
I have given so little and taken so much.
The night, an indifferent witness, covers me in ancillary blackness.
I talk myself up and down.
A monarch butterfly undulates beneath the Victorian love seat.
Sleep with me.
We must get back to a beauty that is not of our own making.

Larger Sea

In the dream, I am beholden to a light as if entering the same
doorway over and over.
                        Two yellow oranges on a brick stoop,
            fallen from the tree, deliberately placed
and then forgotten.

My throat was slit but I went on talking to the silence,
                        interrogating myself, forcing myself to
            believe one idea after the next,
because they seemed like good ideas.

ii.
Sad, really. The days becoming the larger sea. In the dream: a
            basket of brightly colored paper. The
papers contain fortunes, messages, lessons.

I stare into an empty bowl, the color of a chlorinated pool.

Why limit the self by subject? Subject being a reflection of
            perception always fleeting
and untrustworthy.

*The mind runs across the plane of memory. Statue of Divine
            Mother. Statue of St. Francis.*
Statue of a girl holding two birds and an empty water jug.

What you see is the self, in aspect.

Then I was free. Why grieve one meaning over another? The
            little towns of your sorrow
                        are behind you, bound to the past.
Dissociate from them and risk knowing yourself.

Slicing Beets

fuchsia splattering and the morning like a tide of light in the window

outside the sea recalls

one slender iris shouting out into negative space
what I see today is emptiness around the life

but life, too

the feminine body a pod

last year's parched and coiled geraniums,
no release from memory

the beginning apricot blossoms like white sparks

sliced in half, the beet has trunk-like rings
—a stain of itself in the inner body

O inaudible digression: *I never wanted children*

until the plausible absence has weight—sting of prophecy

White-Tailed Deer Feeding

What struck me was their disregard, the cropped tails like
        bunched flags,
how they stood poised and balanced on the hillside.

It was docile, too, the slow deliberate feeding into early evening.

At first, the doe appeared to be alone
among the white flowering bushes, her neck a perfect
        geometrical arc.

You think I wanted it this way?
The failed marriage like a mar.

I have gone on, in the face of an emptiness I wish on no one.

So the bride? Her dress, a bloody drape.
You get the idea.

I think I am like that doe in the imagined aloneness,
the way I cut myself off from the world to get away from you.

I look up, and there are more feeding, one behind the rocks,
another near the jacaranda, and the sun, omphalic,

is lost behind the hill.

Elegy

Leaving the marriage was like being left by my father, and below that a separate self, a girl on ice.

Do you think I haven't been here before? Cowering before your absence, convincing myself I can't go on.

The waves turn gun metal under the boisterous sky.
I am taking the anvil of my own undoing and throwing it back at you,
walking up and down the shore, entirely alone, entirely alone.
Could she have been more perfect?

Ignoring the rumors, the hearsay, the signs: the single lace stocking crammed in a ball under a pile of papers.

OK. I agreed to remain untouched because it was what I had to do
        to keep you.
Look the other way. I did (my part).

It was what my father asked of me before he left my mother.
The way blame became a target I drew around myself, in order to
        accommodate you.

Resilience

plunged into light, and the refrain of absence, which is another way
of saying,
I gave up. Pointillism of stars, seen and unseen.

A whole year lost like being buried in the ground, fetal and living.

You: a rudder, a governor. Remind me: I walked away.

The mind and its cataclysms. Before that, the morning glory torn from
the fence. Because I missed even
the small attachments. Heartily, it came back as promised, tilting green
leaves like saucers towards
the sun. Look up, look up, they seem to say, drawn to light and warmth.

Buried rings. My mother tells me, *When I divorced your father I buried
my wedding ring.* Where? On
the top of the ridge.

Years. Motel curtains. Other people's houses. Displacement. What was I
being taught?

Pulleys and vines of sleep. Agreement to go under. Spelling it out with
touch in the palm, because I
refused words.

Quotidian

Red dress servitude after-myth or you could say
Sleeping lover / tomb baby (I) no longer break accepting
absence

still seedlings as much underground as above.

She is homeless. Her feet calloused ashy as a coalwalker
under the Guatemalan colored blanket that will break the
I. These problems don't fade.

Maybe offer her a trip to detox. Freeway littered with telephone
        books like a flock of birds.
Moving shadows the Los Angeles morning, too-fast traffic
        on Lincoln

a crow shrugs under its wings like Dracula pulling up his cape
human feces in the alley against the cheery cantaloupe brick wall.

She moves on. Attribute the whole social weight to lack of
        spiritual climax.

Upstairs my friend sleeps and wakes. Leafless nameless tree
        opened nursery rhyme pie.

After Marriage

An orange butterfly oscillating
over the stone Buddha and the potted
geraniums;

its wings like hands making a shadow puppet of a bird, only no
wall, the sky seamless.

In the correspondence between spaces we are returned to ourselves.

Which direction to go? Clouds busted up, moving across the
bluest sky—a dislodged puzzle
in a field of light.

I wanted to be sealed in again, not to acknowledge the
responsibility of choices.

In the end is no way to preface what I want to say, as if marriage,
even a failed one, ever truly ends.

After all, you'd like to remind me, I was the one who left
and I could list a thousand reasons why.

The sustained trauma: leaving was being left.
Little oscillating butterfly, the color of a heat coil and the struggle
for place.

It was the smallest window. More light came through. Too
much light.

Three years and two lovers later, I still go back to you
as if I need the wall we built between us to sustain me.

White Torch

Blood on my finger in a theater of loss, buried overnight in the
        yellowest flower.
                And the path black, dropped lower and lower.

Maybe *utter abandon* would save you. Calla lily blooming unexpectedly
                in a ditch of weeds, white torch, frozen form,
not yet spring, molecular beginning, as if for the first time.
Did you think there would be no opposition? *Utter abandon.*

Even now I want to call on you, black sprig of self-denial.
Sparrows on the red fence. The impatiens, bright and gleaming
        like gift wrap in the sun.

I have stood in the doorway to some other world made
        luminous by grief
                and been brought to this moment.

Elegy

We trawl the lake for faces and for luck, for exposition. Across
        the thoroughfare
is the safe house of memory, just an apple and a spool of rue,
        so don't get too excited.

Using a manual alphabet verifies any and all inadequacy.

I have learned to hurt and take shortcuts.
The stairs the alto sings into being are always covered in snow.

Elegy

The morning is a buried place.
Come back, so I can take you in.

More than I can count, blackbirds' dominion
above the cornfield, high above the cornfield.
More than I can count.

The pile of rocks is dangerous, because we won't listen
to sympathy or tenderness. I've told you that, right?

How incongruous desire is to truth, and how the dot-to-dot
of imaginary expanse is just that: *imaginary*.

Safety and Memory

the place between being and not being, the place between
        wanting and not
               the carcass of a dog laid against the curb on
        Marmion Way, (today) you passed twice
and each time a little of you died too—

a man on a bike with large straw hat looking at the dog

sun white like God, sun high and white and strong

the place between, interval . . .

you were in the presumed safety of your car, the palm trees along
        Rodeo decorated for Christmas
with banners of angels, blue silver flags

between what you imagined and where you are . . .
        most importantly *being*
sorrow was, in part, the defiance of expectations

memory: watching the family Irish setter get hit by a car, spinning in
        manic circles and the way

your father carried her to the back of the camper, already knowing
        she was dead

Variation on Seeing: A Prayer

Maybe rivulets. Maybe a little loss.
The disproportionate attachments left like broken toys in a box.

I come to you in reverence.

Flaming arrow to the heart, cliché said, the dream voice and you
        were writing to Christ.
Maybe, even outside of understanding. Maybe, even to the tangible
        presence which was your own being
reflected back at you.

If. About matter and not about matter. Early morning rim of sun
        and your consciousness touching
everywhere, extending into the gorgeous purple, into the
        halting orange.

By then longing had me, longing and memory. As a child I . . .
        Amulet of sun.

To speak of joining, that separateness I imposed to make it
        through, to get by.

Even in language, a pure love of the fragment, the thing cut off
        and incomplete.

Hand. Lip. Cup. Breast. Letter. Rose garden. Moon over palm trees.

Wasn't there weight to be carried? Didn't it begin with the body?
        Didn't it begin with desire?
To disallow narrative, so that the image embodies the story.

Fuchsia bougainvillea like a hat on the roof. The original sky. The
        sky so infinite, the *you* happily
lost. All the old doors no longer there, and the new—possible—
        this variation of seeing.

Everywhere

Everywhere to me everywhere, everywhere to me I'm calling your number,
I'm calling your number, everywhere to me
　　　　　　　　　　　　　　　　　—Bran Van 3000

i.
All morning long I have watched my dog race the perimeter of
　　　　the fence in an instinctual frenzy

　　　　　　　　　　　—a baby possum huddled on a cement
　　　　ledge in the neighbor's yard, his rat tail
showing from underneath the banana leaf—just inches out of reach.

Only in the form of addiction could the river cut into your hand.
Call up your ex-husband. Call up an ex-lover.

And each day numbered,
　　　　　　　　　　—the ledge untrustworthy, a steep incline below.
I poked a broken pencil through
the fence, prodding the possum's small body, hoping to push it off or
　　　　scare it—

because I couldn't take the dog's dumbfounded urgency,
　　　　his relentlessness
　　　　　　　　　　to get at what couldn't be gotten.

ii.
O house on fire. O set up. Did you think you were through with
　　　　the rage?
The body of the mother, the mother body, so syrupy.

Blue veils fall like living sky.

Palm trees, umbrella-like, the need for shelter
and everything endlessly burning.

65

Left in the black margins of addiction and longing and no relief
the doubt came in your other voice, the voice of *you cannot be*

it was larger than unworthiness to stand at the edge of the yard,
right before it goes wild, overtaken by foxtails

and weeds gangly in their sea of formlessness.

Eventually, I left them—the dog, pulling at the fence, whining
        in frustration;
the possum, stupefied as a decoy in its fright.

The need for release is greater than
plastic icons, momentary pleasure.

Haven't you had enough? The river bleeding, the river less
        painful than the life below.
The river of the body, the river of swollen incantation,

the river where you are obliterated over and over
by your own need to be left.

The men come and go, they rise phosphorescent—desire
        molecular as ice.

Love Poem to My Grandmother

Those last weeks of my grandmother's life I came in from L.A.
        to say goodbye.
Meals like child's play, the miniature portions
grouped on the white side plate, the can of chocolate Ensure
        near the lamp.

                        Unrecognizable bird of being your song
            falls off into space
over the flowering jade whose rays
                    splinter experience into consciousness.

She sat in an armchair too weak to speak, too weak to lift a fork
        to her mouth,
                    a band of oxygen tubing under her nose,
while effervescent sounds from its tank hummed
like a far-off waterfall until we *were anointed in light.*

It was a sound patterned from the eternal.
                I fed her red grapes and bits of honeydew,
        the only foods she had any interest in,
while she slipped in and out of consciousness.
                        berries bejeweled like astral stars
        or stains of matter

Asking for a cigarette. Talking to the long-dead. Asking for
        her sewing.
The struggle for breath, the way she moved from world to world,
        it was all effort;

                    not yet wholly spirit, and body breaking
        down, so there was some suffering.

                    Among *the slow yield of temporal experience,*
we sat in silence. My grandma slouched and humpback.
Even now I can hear my own voice divided,

stunned by loss and abject brilliance.

Outside it was fall in Sandwich, Illinois. I kicked up leaves.
They fell in a panoply of rusts and oranges.

I was in her aqua parka, marked with flesh-toned make-up
          around the collar.
It smelled like her, part Avon, part Estée Lauder.

There was a rift inside me,
my soul rushing to memorize this form, this face,
every last wrinkle, every scar, to touch one last time what I could
          still understand,

the scattered lights, the wind constant, all that is earthbound
          and called back.

Building and Dwelling

i.
And then the central darkness was over, all the offshoots of
        desire, their beams of radiance
like filaments from the sun.

Some days you caught yourself in love with the world, the lizard
        like a miniature dragon
asleep in the light, its particular inclusion on the pavement.

Twice in a row—doves mating, the lack of concision
            —wings flapping, one bird moving away
—high on the telephone wire—they seemed off-balance, but
        driven together.

Later the clownish squirrel bounding over the rod iron steeples
        of a neighbor's fence, a little Tarzan
grabbing for a leafy limb.

Wasn't it all instinct? So what set you apart was the conscious
        choices of your longing?

ii.
The lightning like a photographer's flash, before and after
        morning thunder
what we called *angels bowling*

that was a long time ago, long enough it's possible to speak of
        brevity and loss
or memory's coil as part of the teeming world lit with new rain

and the emptiness you cannot separate yourself from

the emptiness of beginnings and the ex-husband, whose face
        you barely remember,
whose name you no longer call out

iii.
What the bird heard, artificer to the morning. Already the momentum
of summer heat building—shock of daylight.

What the bird heard. An answer back? Its own catalog of song?
The chug of a truck up the hill.

What the bird heard. The sound pleased you, his song pleased you
walking up the hill, heading into your understanding
                            of what it means to be alive,
breath, song, body.

Revelatory Borders

Early evening Bethlehem light so shallow anyone can see
            through your skin
that's how the door opened by claiming borders

Electric hows and whys luminous like veins on a face
Walled city of joy exclamation of a smile

Always having the flood to push / invent now there's an excursion
It was the wall of touch making vistas
as in plane of understanding and hope, desultory falling

feather like when a pillow get(s) fluffed there's always innocence
here *love* remains not who you have but *what* you are

lesson: *other* from that understanding

Notes

1) The epigram at the beginning of the book is from Letter 600, "a fragment seemingly clipped from a letter or a draft of a letter" to Otis P. Lord, written by Emily Dickinson about 1879; 2) In "Libation Bowl with Acorns and Bees," the gold phiale artefact referred to is on display at The Metropolitan Museum of Art. A faint Greek inscription on the bowl gives the beginning of a name, "Pausi . . ."; 3) "Demane and Demazana" is based on an African folk tale about a brother and sister, twins and orphans, who run away from home and encounter a cannibal who tries to catch them. Demazana is tricked and caught, but, while the cannibal prepares the fire, her brother substitutes a sack of bees for his sister and the cannibal is outwitted. He turns into a tree forever, where the bees make their hive; 4) "Mother of the Waters" was inspired by Diane Wolkstein's retelling of the Haitian folktale "Mother of the Waters," from her book *The Magic Orange Tree and Other Haitian Folktales;* 5) The epigram and title of "Everywhere" are from a song by Bran Van 3000, also titled "Everywhere" (produced by Haig V. for A Zoobone Sound / Bob Power / EP Bergen and Bran Man; © 1998 Audiogram Records; manufactured by Capitol Records, Inc.).

photo by Muriel Mutzel

Gretchen Mattox was born in Denver, Colorado, and educated at the University of Colorado, New York University, and Columbia University. She has been a fellow at the Virginia Center for the Creative Arts, the Edward Albee Foundation, and Yaddo, as well as an instructor at The New School for Social Research, Antioch University, and Loyola Marymount University. She lives in Los Angeles, California, where she co-edits *Pool*.

New Issues Poetry & Prose

Editor, Herbert Scott

Vito Aiuto, *Self-Portrait as Jerry Quarry*
James Armstrong, *Monument In A Summer Hat*
Michael Burkard, *Pennsylvania Collection Agency*
Anthony Butts, *Fifth Season*
Kevin Cantwell, *Something Black in the Green Part of Your Eye*
Gladys Cardiff, *A Bare Unpainted Table*
Kevin Clark, *In the Evening of No Warning*
Jim Daniels, *Night with Drive-By Shooting Stars*
Joseph Featherstone, *Brace's Cove*
Lisa Fishman, *The Deep Heart's Core Is a Suitcase*
Robert Grunst, *The Smallest Bird in North America*
Robert Haight, *Emergences and Spinner Falls*
Mark Halperin, *Time as Distance*
Myronn Hardy, *Approaching the Center*
Edward Haworth Hoeppner, *Rain Through High Windows*
Cynthia Hogue, *Flux*
Janet Kauffman, *Rot* (fiction)
Josie Kearns, *New Numbers*
Maurice Kilwein Guevara, *Autobiography of So-and-so: Poems in Prose*
Ruth Ellen Kocher, *When the Moon Knows You're Wandering*
Steve Langan, *Freezing*
Lance Larsen, *Erasable Walls*
David Dodd Lee, *Downsides of Fish Culture*
Deanne Lundin, *The Ginseng Hunter's Notebook*
Joy Manesiotis, *They Sing to Her Bones*
Sarah Mangold, *Household Mechanics*
David Marlatt, *A Hog Slaughtering Woman*
Gretchen Mattox, *Goodnight Architecture*
Paula McLain, *Less of Her*
Sarah Messer, *Bandit Letters*
Malena Mörling, *Ocean Avenue*
Julie Moulds, *The Woman with a Cubed Head*
Marsha de la O, *Black Hope*

C. Mikal Oness, *Water Becomes Bone*
Elizabeth Powell, *The Republic of Self*
Margaret Rabb, *Granite Dives*
Rebecca Reynolds, *Daughter of the Hangnail; The Bovine Two-Step*
Martha Rhodes, *Perfect Disappearance*
Beth Roberts, *Brief Moral History in Blue*
John Rybicki, *Traveling at High Speeds*
Mary Ann Samyn, *Inside the Yellow Dress*
Mark Scott, *Tactile Values*
Martha Serpas, *Côte Blanche*
Diane Seuss-Brakeman, *It Blows You Hollow*
Marc Sheehan, *Greatest Hits*
Sarah Jane Smith, *No Thanks—and Other Stories* (fiction)
Phillip Sterling, *Mutual Shores*
Angela Sorby, *Distance Learning*
Russell Thorburn, *Approximate Desire*
Rodney Torreson, *A Breathable Light*
Robert VanderMolen, *Breath*
Martin Walls, *Small Human Detail in Care of National Trust*
Patricia Jabbeh Wesley, *Before the Palm Could Bloom: Poems of Africa*